Johnson's®

learning to talk

London, New York, Munich, Melbourne, Delhi

Text by Professor James Law
For Jane, Isla and Euan

Senior editors Julia North, Salima Hirani
Senior art editor Hannah Moore
Project editor Esther Ripley
Project art editor Ann Burnham
DTP designer Karen Constanti
Production controller Heather Hughes
Managing editors Anna Davidson, Liz Coghill
Managing art editor Glenda Fisher
Photography art direction Sally Smallwood
Photography Ruth Jenkinson

Publishing director Corinne Roberts

First published in Great Britain in 2004 by
Dorling Kindersley, A Penguin Company
80 Strand, London, WC2R 0RL

Every effort has been made to ensure that the information contained in this book is complete and
accurate. However, neither the publisher nor the author are engaged in rendering professional advice or
services to the individual reader. The ideas, procedures and suggestions contained in this book are not
intended as a substitute for consulting with your healthcare provider. All matters regarding the health of
you and your baby require medical supervision. Neither the author nor the publisher shall be liable or
responsible for any loss or damage allegedly arising from any information or suggestion in this book.

A CIP catalogue record for this book is available from the British Library

ISBN 0 7513 3888 5

Reproduced by Colourscan, Singapore
Printed by Star Standard, Singapore

See our complete catalogue at
www.dk.com

A message to parents from

Johnson's®

The most precious gift in the world is a new baby. To your little one, you are the centre of the universe. And by following your most basic instincts to touch, hold and talk to your baby, you provide the best start to a happy, healthy life.

Our baby products encourage parents to care for and nurture their children through the importance of touch, developing a deep, loving bond that transcends all others.

Parenting is not an exact science, nor is it a one–size–fits–all formula. For more than a hundred years, Johnson & Johnson has supported the healthcare needs of parents and healthcare professionals, and we understand that all parents feel more confident in their role when they have information they can trust.

That is why we offer this book as our commitment to you to provide scientifically sound, professionally reviewed guidance on the important topics of pregnancy, babycare and child development.

As you read through this book, the most important thing to remember is this: you know your baby better than anyone else. By watching, listening and having confidence in your natural ability, you will know how to use the information you have in your hands, for the benefit of the baby in your arms.

Contents

" Almost from the word go I felt Sarah was teaching us how **to interact** with her. She showed us exactly how she felt and it was not long before she was telling us **what to do, too.** "

JOSH is dad to three-year-old Sarah

1

The miracle of speech

Learning to talk is one of the most amazing things that children do – but it happens so automatically you may never give much thought to how your baby accomplishes it. Within a few years your crying newborn baby becomes an engaging companion asking questions, telling stories and letting you know exactly how she feels.

An amazing potential

People have always been intrigued about why and how babies learn to speak. In the space of three or four years children pick up virtually all the essentials of a spoken language, apparently without conscious effort or formal lessons. Anyone who has struggled to learn a second language at school or later in life will find it hard to imagine how they do that.

All babies learn language, and they do so at the same rate whether they speak English, Spanish, Tagalog, Gujarati or French. Language is an innate characteristic of humans and the potential for it is present in all babies at birth, although exactly what the nature of that potential is remains a puzzle.

What we do know is that children learn language so quickly it is clear that they must be born with some kind of mechanism that allows it to happen. The remarkable changes that allow language to develop begin very early in a baby's life, but language skills carry on developing right through to adolescence.

Your part in the process

At first, your baby can do little more than alert you to her needs by crying, but her brain is ready wired to start making sense of language sounds. What she needs is stimulation, and lots of it, from the people around her. Your attention, interest and conversation provide everything she needs to get started.

Most parents don't really need to be told how to interact with their children. It's likely that you began to do so within minutes of your baby's birth as you greeted her face-to-face for the first time and welcomed her to the world. What this book sets out to do is enhance an interaction that comes naturally, to enrich the experience for you both.

Why talk matters

Talking to children matters. In a recent study, researchers identified a noticeable decline in language skills in three year olds in the UK. They believe that many children are starting nursery without ever having had one-to-one conversations.

The concern is that parents are not spending enough time talking to their children, possibly because they are relying too much on toys, television and computer games that entertain without adult interaction. To become able talkers, children need one-to-one practice and lots of good examples of talk.

The basics of talk

Most of the time we communicate so effortlessly, we fail to appreciate how complex human communication is. However, to understand how children learn to talk, it helps to separate out some of its different elements: these are communication, language and speech.

Beginning to communicate

It seems that children are born not just to speak but also to interact with other people – their parents in the first instance but soon everyone else around them. Long before your baby uses words, she uses cries and gestures to make her meaning clear and responds to and learns to read the gestures and facial expressions of those who care for her.

At first, your interaction with your baby is made up of stroking, rocking, smiling and eye contact – gestures that convey your feelings more effectively than words can. They tell your baby that you love her and are interested in her. She understands emotion long before she can talk.

GESTURES
Smiles, touch and eye contact tell your baby you are interested in who she is.

Gestures, facial expression and body language are a major part of communication in these early months and continue to be so throughout life. Think how much you use them to enhance your speech and interpret what you hear. They are an essential fall back when a meaning is unclear or a language is foreign to you.

However, human communication is also about referring to and describing the world, and this is the next step your child takes towards becoming a talker. Once she has established what words do and how they relate to things, it is only a matter of time before she is naming what she sees – "woof", "bus", "drink" and "mum".

What is language?

Language in general, and grammar in particular, is what distinguishes humans from other animals. This system we have of combining words into meaningful sequences enables us to give shape to our ideas and thoughts and convey them to others.

One of the really distinctive features of our capacity to learn language is our ability to be creative with sentences. Although we use some expressions over and over again, we are constantly producing new sentences that we have never said before and that we have never heard anyone else say either.

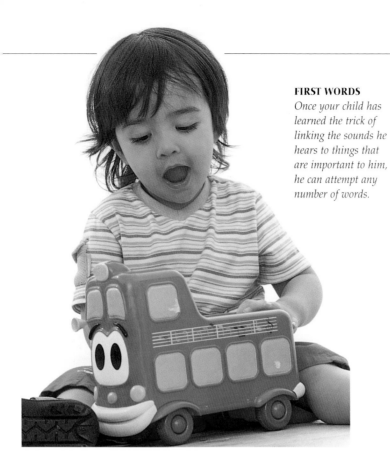

FIRST WORDS
Once your child has learned the trick of linking the sounds he hears to things that are important to him, he can attempt any number of words.

Checklist

Language is made up of:

● phonemes such as /b/ and /p/ – the smallest sound units of language. They are speech sounds not letters and there are about 40 in English

● morphemes – the smallest meaningful unit of language. "Do" is a morpheme but so is "un" because it changes or adds meaning

● syntax – the combination of words into phrases and sentences.

Can other creatures talk?

Do any animals other than humans have language? Observers of animal communication have made some fascinating discoveries.

● The North American cicada has four different calls, each one with a different message. The vervet monkey has 36 calls.

● Bees dance in a pattern to direct other bees to nearby pollen supplies.

● Dolphins can communicate specific information to other dolphins.

● Mynah birds and parrots mimic speech but there is no evidence that they can understand any of it.

● Chimpanzees and gorillas are the only animals with anything that resembles a human capacity for communication. They do not have the vocal apparatus to speak but they can be taught to communicate using sign language, keyboards and cards. In teaching programmes, some have learned to use hundreds of signs and understand even more.

However, even the cleverest gorillas and chimpanzees are able to form only the most basic sentences. They do not come close to being as creative with language as the average two-year-old human being.

By two and a half, most children are using the three main components of a complex language system. They learn the rules of *phonology* as they combine sounds into words. Then they get to grips with *syntax* as they combine words in the correct order to make up phrases and sentences such as "Get ball" or "Pasta all gone". Although these are simple requests and observations, they are *semantic* (they have a precise meaning). In fact children start to put words together as soon as they want to communicate more complicated meanings.

Children's language skills are not simply confined to what they are able to say – they also need to understand what they hear. An essential part of learning to talk is using what they know about language to work out what others are saying.

When does learning to talk begin?

A baby's first experiences with sounds begin in the womb. In the last weeks of pregnancy the pathways in the brain that allow hearing are already well developed, and babies begin to recognize sounds they hear often, especially their mother's voice. They sometimes kick strongly in response to a loud noise or become still when soft music is played.

Fascinating research

Babies in the womb can learn to recognize a wide range of sounds – even a story if it is read to them often enough. In one study, a group of newborns showed that they could recognize Dr Seuss' *The Cat in the Hat*, after their mothers were asked to read the story aloud twice a day during the last six weeks of pregnancy. In another study, newborns responded to the theme tune of a soap opera that their mums watched every day. No one suggests that babies can learn to talk in the womb, but research shows they are equipped to start learning from you at birth.

After birth

Once your baby is born the process of learning to talk is closely linked to her social development. She must want to communicate and this may not be automatic in all children. In most cases, what makes your baby want to talk is *you*.

SOUNDS BEFORE BIRTH
Towards the end of your pregnancy try playing a piece of music to your baby every day during a quiet moment. You may find she is soothed by it after the birth.

FACE TO FACE
Your face, your smile and the sound of your voice mean everything to your young baby. Watching and listening to you speak and making her own sounds in response puts her on the path to becoming a talker herself.

★ At first, she is fascinated by your face and gazes at your eyes and mouth while you make the sounds she likes so much. She uses body language and smiles to show that she is pleased to see you.
★ Next, she has to listen for the sounds of speech all around her and start trying them out herself. Then she has to make associations between the sounds that we call words and what they refer to. This means that, at the very least, she must be able to remember what she has seen and heard.
★ Becoming mobile is often the final spur to speech because it broadens her experience. Now she has so much more to tell you, she has an even greater drive to communicate.

BROADENING HORIZONS
When your baby can cross a floor and fetch something to show you, he usually wants to try to tell you about it, too.

Finding her voice

Your baby's first sounds tend to be nasal because her voice box (larynx) is high up close to her mouth, and her throat (pharynx) is short. She becomes able to make speech sounds as her larynx descends and her pharynx lengthens. This is happening rapidly by the end of her first year and is complete by age three.

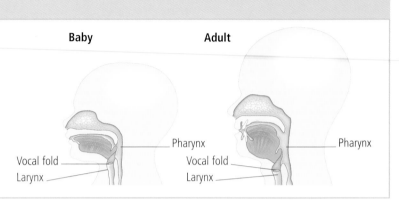

Baby   **Adult**

Pharynx

Vocal fold

Larynx

Pharynx

Vocal fold

Larynx

Practising her speech

Your baby's speech is made up of phonemes – all the sounds of the language or languages that she is learning in her first year, usually from her mum and dad. The earliest sounds she makes are not specific to any language but, by 12 months or so, she is already specializing in the ones she will need to use.

Making speech sounds is not an easy task for a baby and relies as much on her physical development as her growing ability to think. She has to be able to control her head, bring her lips together deliberately, move her tongue up and down and use the soft palate at the top of her mouth to produce them. All of this has to be coordinated with her breathing and the movement of her voice box (larynx). To begin with your baby will have little control over this, but by her first birthday she will be producing a range of sounds that are more and more like real speech. Soon she will be producing her first attempts at words.

Critical time?

Do children have to learn language at a particular stage in their life, and is the chance lost for ever if they are not given enough stimulation?

No scientist would prevent a child from learning language, so answers to these questions have to be based on rare examples of children who have been raised in isolation with no meaningful contact with humans. From these studies it appears that a child who is not exposed to language in the first eight or nine years is very unlikely to learn language.

Although language learning is innate, it appears to rely on experiences during key periods for its development. The first six months of life seem to be critical for homing

SOUND PLAY
She loves to practise sounds, and uses them with all the variety and expression of real speech as she chats to her toys and "reads" from her books.

" Sam got to his feet and began to tell everyone about the circus we had seen. He remembered so much detail. I couldn't believe how confident he was. "

TESS is mum to four-year-old Sam

in on the sounds of the child's native language, and in the years between one and five, grammar is more easily acquired than at any other time in life. There is evidence, too, that a child's early talking skills continue to have a bearing on the way the brain is configured once it becomes more specialized in language during adolescence.

What is certain is that the first three years of life are a critically important learning period for children. After the first year, language is the key that helps children unlock many of their discoveries about the world, enables them to order and express their thoughts and ideas, and opens the door to literacy.

Talking milestones

Babies acquire speech skills in the same order, whatever their language. These are the stages your baby passes through en route to becoming a talker.

● She makes non-verbal sounds and uses intonation to express what she wants. She points to ask for things or makes a noise to get attention.

● She uses her own versions of words that are understood within the family, for example, "bi-bi" becomes the family word for biscuit. The rise and fall of her voice is still very important in letting you know what she means.

● She begins to use and speak her first conventional words.

● She uses single words to mean more than the thing she is referring to. For example "drink" begins to mean "Can you get me a drink?"

● She uses two words together: "Mummy gone" or "More ball". Although she knows what she means, some phrases are not obvious to unfamiliar listeners and need to be deciphered by trial and error.

● She combines two or three words to make sentences that include an object or person (a noun) and something happening (a verb) – "Dog eat dinner".

● She links ideas using conjunctions such as "and" and uses word endings such as "ed" to make different tenses.

" Hannah started using her first words – she called our dog 'woof' – just before her **first birthday** but I had a strong sense that she had been building up to those **words for months. "**

JACK is dad to 18-month-old Hannah

Smiles, babbles & words

From the moment your baby is born, and often before, you will notice his reactions to voices and other sounds. Over the coming months he will become a collector of all the information he needs to produce his first words. The quest begins as soon as he is born because learning about the joys of human interaction has its roots in the first few weeks of life when you and your baby start to get to know one another.

The drive to communicate

Your newborn baby may seem like a small, helpless bundle, but he is an active communicator from the word go. At first, his cries and burps relate only to how he is feeling, whether he is hungry, tired, needs a fresh nappy or has too much wind. Although he doesn't yet know that he is sending out a message, your response teaches him that his cries have consequences – they bring rewards. It's not long before he begins to use crying to express specific needs and focus it on the people who are likely to do something about them. He is already beginning to communicate.

Your first conversations are all about kindness, reassurance and making him feel safe. Most parents chatter away to their babies without really being aware of it: "Hello baby, have you woken up for your feed?"

"Over to Daddy, now – he wants to change your nappy." "Ooh, you don't like me taking off your vest, do you?" To your baby this is nothing more than a meaningless string of sounds, but they make him feel calm and attended to nonetheless.

Using all his senses

Your baby's rapid development in his first year involves all his senses – vision, hearing, touch, taste and smell. As soon as he is born, they help him to know who and what is important to him and gradually over the coming months he is trained to use his senses to gather information. Even if he can hear, he must learn to listen. As soon as he can focus, he needs to learn to direct his attention so he can begin to recognize gestures, facial expressions, familiar objects and movements.

Checklist

Babies pass these talking milestones in their first year:

- cooing after six weeks
- babbling from six months; increasing experimentation with sounds
- begin to use specific sounds in specific contexts, for example "woof" for all animals
- by nine months, understand "no" and "bye"
- by age one, recognize some words and respond to requests such as "clap your hands"; may speak one or two words.

Your baby's cries

Researchers have identified four basic infant cries.

- Birth cry – two gasps followed by a wail that lasts one second.
- Basic cry – a rhythmic pattern of loud crying, followed by silence, a whistling in-breath and a pause, sometimes accompanied by sucking movements.
- Pain cry – a loud, long, shrill cry followed by a long breath-holding silence and short whimpers. Baby tenses facial muscles, frowns and clenches fists.
- Anger cry – a prolonged breath out followed immediately by an exasperated wail.

Your newborn baby can see best at a distance of about 20cm (8in). He prefers light-dark contrasts, such as black patterns on a white background, because these are easier to distinguish than traditional pastels – many first rattles and mobiles are now designed with this in mind.

The sounds he hears best are in the frequency of the human voice, which is why he is predisposed to listen to you as you talk and sing to him. In these first few weeks, hold him just a short distance from your face as you talk to him so he can focus on your eyes and lips. Chat away while you attend to him and keep him nearby when he is awake so he can listen to the rise and fall of voices around him. Make sure there are quiet times in your home with the radio and television turned off so he can develop his listening skills.

First sounds and responses

At first your baby simply cries for attention and makes little snorts, grunts, burping and swallowing noises, but after one week he begins to imitate his own sounds and make little whoops and cries. They are not intended for an audience, but like

HAPPY SMILE
He looks into your eyes and his face breaks into a gummy smile – he is on his way to becoming social.

most parents, you treat them as meaningful and respond anyway.

During his first month your baby will learn to distinguish your voice if you are his main carer. If you call out to him and talk reassuringly when he begins to cry, he may pause momentarily and be calmed by your voice. Loud noises such as a door slamming may alarm him; he freezes all his limbs and then breaks into a distraught wail. He finds prolonged, repetitive noises soothing and may be sent to sleep by your singing or, less flatteringly, to the steady sloshing of the washing machine or the drone of the vacuum cleaner.

YOUR VOICE
Your baby's hearing is attuned to human voices and the voice that he finds most soothing and calming is your own.

First smiles

One of the key parts of interaction between you and your baby is your smile. When he smiles back, it is like a magic ingredient that makes everything work better, especially if your first few weeks with a new baby have been an uphill battle.

At first your baby's fleeting imitations of smiles have not really been under his control nor related to anything in particular, however, by six weeks, his smile is less automatic and he prefers faces to any other visual treat. He meets your gaze when you hold him close and you feel that his lop-sided grin is intended just for you.

Questions & Answers

My daughter's hearing was fine when she was tested at birth but is there a way I can keep a check on it during her first year?
Your baby will have a second hearing test check at around seven months (see Hearing Tests, p.57) but the following signs will reassure you that she is hearing normally.

Shortly after birth – she is startled by a sudden loud noise such as a hand clap or a door slamming.

By 1 month – she pauses and listens to prolonged sounds such as the noise of a vacuum cleaner.

By 4 months – she quietens or smiles at the sound of your voice even when she cannot see you. She may turn her head or eyes towards you if you approach quietly from behind and speak to her from the side.

By 7 months – she turns to very quiet noises made on either side of her if she is not too absorbed with her toys.

By 9 months – she listens attentively to everyday sounds and searches for very quiet sounds made out of sight. She shows pleasure in babbling loudly and tunefully.

By 12 months – she now shows a response to several familiar words. She may respond to "no" and "bye-bye", even when there is no accompanying gesture.

Baby linguists

When someone speaks a language that is foreign to your baby, see how alert and interested he becomes.

From birth to around six months of age, babies have an extraordinary language ability. Researchers have shown that newborns can make fine distinctions between sounds in their native language, such as "pa" and "ba", but even more remarkably can detect changes in sounds in other languages – everything from Chinese tones to African clicks. No language outwits them. When the babies detect a difference they suck harder on a dummy attached to a computer that records the strength and frequency of their sucking.

It seems that, early on, babies have the potential to learn any language. Japanese babies, for example, can distinguish between the sounds "l" and "r" in English, something adult Japanese find difficult. All babies, however, lose this "ear" for other languages by the age of one when they are fully focused on the sounds of their own language.

Becoming sociable

When you speak to your six-week-old baby he responds with whole body movements – a stretching and jiggling that tells you he is interested and excited. You feel flattered, but soon realize he is likely to make the same response when a mobile is blown by a breeze or sunlight plays across the bars of his cot. But by three months he is becoming much more sociable. He is now focused on people and will often pay more attention to your face than he will to another less interesting task, such as

BABY MIMIC
Your five-month-old can mimic expressions if you exaggerate them and then wait for her to try them herself.

feeding, especially when he is not particularly hungry. He pauses from the bottle or breast to grin happily at you and ventures a few sounds to gain your attention.

By five months he can mimic expressions, something you may discover inadvertently if he catches you mid-yawn. Test him out by sticking out your tongue or drawing your mouth into a round "oooh" – then pause to see if he copies you.

At six months, babies are suddenly much more aware of the difference between familiar and strange and may be wary of people they don't know. Your baby greets anyone familiar or special to him with a beaming smile of welcome and is becoming a rewarding playmate.

Communicating by touch

While you play and talk to your baby don't underestimate the value of stroking, touch and massage, which, research shows, are as important to the wellbeing of babies and young children as sleeping and eating. Touch not only makes your baby happy and strengthens the bond between you, it has also been shown to have powerful effects on sleep, behaviour, growth and learning. Although all forms of gentle stroking are good for your baby, you can learn specific techniques from a book or in a class (see page 62).

Playing with sounds

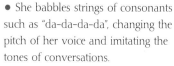

Your baby's early random noises are slowly shaped into strings of sound known as babble. Babbling becomes increasingly sophisticated as your baby gets closer and closer to words. What stage is your baby at?

● She makes delightful cooing noises like a dove, using vowel sounds – "aah", "eeeh" and "oooh". She practises in her cot in the morning or before she falls asleep.

● She adds consonants so "aaah" becomes "baa" or "daa". She now seeks someone to talk to, and turns her head to a voice. She laughs.

● She babbles strings of consonants such as "da-da-da-da", changing the pitch of her voice and imitating the tones of conversations.

● After six months she produces a string of sounds such as "a-a, muh, goo, der, adah, er-leh, aroo" in one breath with changes in pitch, volume and speed. She follows conversations like a spectator at a tennis match.

● Sometimes she automatically repeats something exactly as she hears it, but this is not yet speech.

She squeals with excitement and changes the tone of her babbling when she is unhappy or delighted.

● By nine months, she produces strings of syllables – "dad-dad, adaba mam-mam, agaga." She copies clicks, coughs, hisses and raspberries. Her chatter rises and falls like speech but does not yet have language behind it.

How should I talk to my baby?

Babies become better talkers if they are spoken to a great deal by their parents and carers, but it's not simply a matter of the amount of speech they hear. There is a characteristic way in which most people talk to babies that helps them to focus on and absorb the sounds and words of a language. Experts call it "parentese" or "caregiver talk".

What is parentese?

Do parents need to be instructed in parentese? Most likely not at all. Just as your baby came into the world wired and ready to learn a language, your response to him seems to be programmed, too. You instinctively adjust your tone and style of language to suit his needs. Most grandparents do it quite naturally, too, and even young children seem to know that they have to change their speech when they are addressing babies and younger children. Here are the key features:

★ You speak in a higher-pitched voice and more slowly than normal, with clear pauses at the end of your sentences.

TIME FOR A TALK
The best time for a talk is when your baby is wide awake but not hungry and looks ready to play.

A FRIENDLY GREETING

Move in close when you start the conversation so he can focus on your face and meet your gaze. Start off the conversation with a broad smile and a question – "Hello my beautiful Toby, are you all nice and clean now that you've had your bath?"

PAUSE AND WAIT

Now pause and wait. He may just look straight into your face with a big smile at first because it takes him a little while to work up his own response – perhaps a noise, a body movement or a wave of the hands. If he is beginning to coo or babble, he may offer a string of sounds.

TIMING YOUR REPLY

Either copy his sounds or comment on them, "Oh, that was a good whoop." Don't leave it too long before you reply – he may lose the connection between what you say and what he did, and the dialogue will be broken. Keep the conversation going until his interest begins to wane and he looks away.

★ You exaggerate your intonation, adopting a sing-song voice that emphasizes important words.

★ Your sentences are short, simple and grammatical and also tend to be very repetitive.

★ You repeat back what your child has said or "recast" it to make it a little more complicated. Your baby says "shoe" and you respond with "Yes, you're putting on your shoe – it's a blue shoe".

★ Your vocabulary is "concrete" in that it tends to refer to people or things that are present rather than ideas and things that cannot be seen.

The dance of interaction

First dialogues with your baby may only last a few minutes, but they contain some essential ingredients of conversation – good listening and turn taking. So the next time you ask your baby a question that you assume will be rhetorical, wait for a moment and see if he has something to tell you in return (between two and seven seconds is the ideal pause). Not everyone gets the timing right at first, and babies are often thwarted in their first attempts at conversation. They get an enthusiastic welcome from a visitor, who then looks away to talk to someone else at the critical moment when they are just working up to waving their arms or offering an expressive grunt by way of a reply.

Babies love rituals that follow a set pattern and allow them to take control. When a conversation is working well it is like a dance of interaction where both partners know exactly what to expect.

Setting up little dialogues like this is a great way to let your baby know that he is being listened to and is important. He is being acknowledged as a conversational partner and learning that it is worthwhile trying to communicate.

Your baby's name

The very first word that is likely to have meaning for your baby is his own name. He hears it whenever a familiar or new face says "hello" or "goodbye" and it occurs continually in the speech he hears from his parents and carers. Usually by the time he is four or five months old, he understands that his name has a special relevance to him, although it will be some time before he is able to say it himself.

Fine tuning the sounds

Towards the end of his first year, your baby has a whole battery of sounds at his disposal, spoken with all the conviction and variety of real speech. He no longer tolerates being left out of conversations and can now shout to get attention when he is ignored. Babies of this age really like to make their presence felt, especially when everyone else is silent. Solemn occasions in churches are a favourite time to exercise his voice – the echo is very rewarding.

LOOK, JAMES!
Now he recognizes his own name, it is easier to initiate games and chats and direct his attention to interesting sights and activities.

Your response to this sociable little person is changing too. Now it seems positively rude not to address someone who is so obviously ready for conversational give and take.

● Make time to talk directly to your baby, particularly if life is becoming more hectic now that you are back at work. He needs face-to-face talk with lots of emphasis on key labelling words – "your cup", "Daddy's shoes" – rather than a sea of chatter.

● Even if you are not much given to emotional displays, emphasize your gestures and emotions when you talk to him – they give him vital clues to what you are saying.

● Try to understand his gestures and sounds. Follow his gaze and hazard a guess at what he might be labelling as a "bon". He will be thrilled if you hit on the correct thing. Repeat it back to him – "balloon" – and add some detail, but don't expect him to copy the word correctly.

Working up to words

Imagine your six-month-old hears the following: "nowletsseewhatyouve gotuptoohdearyouvegotawetnappypo orbabynowonderyouvebeencryingwe dbetterchangeyou". To understand this stream of sounds, he has to listen carefully and learn to recognize where one word ends and another begins. "Now let's see what you've got up to.

HIDE AND SEEK
Unveiling a hidden toy never fails to surprise, but don't make the game too difficult or add too many variations.

Expert tips

The best games for babies over six months are repetitive and predictable. It helps them to feel in control of events.

● Put a light scarf over your head and ask your baby to "find Mummy". Stay close so he can pull it off and reveal your face. Now drape it lightly over his head and ask "Where's Joey?". He will soon learn to pull it off himself.

● When your baby is 9 or 10 months old cover up a toy within his reach, letting him watch you as you do it. Now ask him to find the toy. Look surprised and delighted and praise him when he does.

● Hold him facing a mirror and point out what you both can see. "These are Joey's eyes." "This is Joey's nose." "This is Mummy's nose." Soon he will be pointing to his own nose on request, or finding the dolly's eyes or the teddy's ears.

Oh dear, you've got a wet nappy. Poor baby, no wonder you've been crying. We'd better change you."

How do babies manage to do that? The answer is that, at first, he may not really break up the speech stream at all. It may just be a wash of interesting and engaging sounds that leave him feeling reassured and attended to. But as his listening skills improve, he begins to extract some important parts from the sounds he is hearing and decode them by comparing them with the dictionary of words he is forming in his head. You give him clues by slowing your speech, exaggerating the boundaries between words and speaking with expression and shifts of intonation.

Baby body language

Babies start to decipher what people around them mean by watching and listening, and what they understand is made up of all sorts of bits of information – what was said, who said it, when it was said and where it was said. They learn that outstretched arms mean "Come here" long before they understand the words that go with the gesture. Although at first it may be difficult to know whether your baby has really understood the message, it's not long before he is using these familiar gestures himself at the

GETTING THE POINT
Now that he can point he can direct your attention to what he desires most.

Checklist

Your baby's body language becomes increasingly expressive during his first year.

- Turns head away from nipple (then spoon) when he has had enough.
- Jiggles arms and legs when happy.
- Looks from adult to toy then back.
- Tugs at your clothing or arm.
- Holds object out to you.
- Points.
- Touches door to ask you to open it.
- Holds up arms to be cuddled.
- Waves "bye-bye". Shakes head to say "no" and nods to say "yes".

appropriate times. He knows that putting his arms out and smiling to you has a specific effect – he will be picked up and cuddled. Yet when a comparative stranger asks for a hug from your 10-month-old baby, he may shake his head vigorously – a gesture that is every bit as effective as verbal language.

Over the previous months, your baby has developed hand-eye coordination and can pick up and examine interesting objects within his reach. By nine months, your baby can follow your finger and look wherever you point. Now you have a useful tool for focusing his attention on interesting events and sights and the fascinating details in his picture books.

Roots of language

Your baby can direct your attention, too. To begin with, he will simply point – "I want it". However, by about 10 months he will point at an object and then to you, and use his own sound for what he wants. The message here is different because it clearly shows he is aware that you know the word that he is using – "I know that you know what I mean". Here we have the roots of spoken language – "reference". Your baby is referring to the world around him. Without this simple shared reference it would be almost impossible for him to learn language at all.

Gradually, babies begin to expect certain words in certain contexts and fix in mind what they mean. By eight months your baby may follow simple instructions, especially if there is a visual cue such as "say bye-bye to Mummy" (plus wave), or "give it to Daddy" (plus an outstretched hand). He soon starts to show that he knows even more words, looking for the cat when it is mentioned in passing or picking up his cup when someone asks for a drink.

A social being

Towards the end of your baby's first year you are left in no doubt that he is fully equipped with almost everything he needs for effective communication.

● He can gesture welcome and rejection, imitate a full range of facial expressions, shout deep disapproval, and then change his tone to convey unrestrained joy.

● He enjoys dancing and romping, clapping games, music and songs, and can produce a few magical little scales and tunes of his own.

● He will imitate some words if he can manage the right sounds but may still have no idea what they mean –

something an older sibling may take advantage of from time to time.

● He may also have one or two odd little words of his own, but often they can only be interpreted by people who know him very well.

In his first year your baby has developed irresistible social skills alongside his language skills, and the two are now becoming enmeshed. He is discovering that speech is a very effective way of being sociable.

READY TO PLAY
Your baby is a more interesting playmate now that he has some social skills.

Expert tips

Start sharing books when your baby is about six months old.

● Choose simple board books with realistic pictures – they are easier for him to recognize than cartoons.

● Don't be put off if he wants to chew the book rather than look at it.

● Point and chat about what you see but stop as soon as he loses interest.

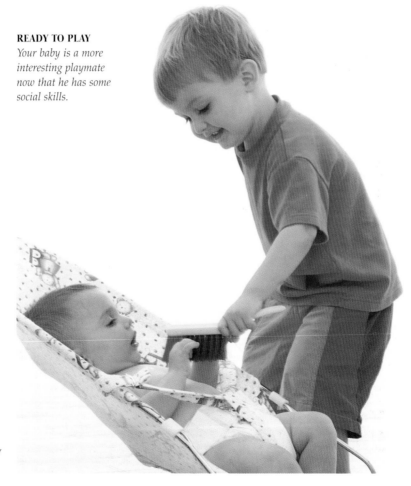

" Ellen used to have conversations with her dolls. She had no more than a handful **of words** but from the way she said them it was clear who **she was copying**. She sounded just like me. "

MYRA is mum to two-year-old Ellen

3

Your toddler can talk

By the end of their first year, many babies begin to say their long-awaited first words. Over the past 12 months they have honed their listening and attention skills and spent many happy hours of practice at coordinating their lips and tongue and making streams of interesting sounds. Most are now fully mobile, either on their knees or their feet, and have a growing number of experiences to talk about.

Your baby's first words

What will your baby's first word be? The chances are this major speech event will refer to something that has excited her, rather than the person who is eagerly waiting for it to happen, so be prepared for it not to be Mum or Dad. Many babies choose to name someone who is absent or an item that has just come into view, for example, a clear "woof" when a dog bounds past the pushchair or "Doey" as big brother Joey leaves the room.

Over the past six months, your baby's passionate interest in people and faces will have diminished in favour of the tantalizing array of objects the world has to offer. She can now handle and explore each new item adeptly and is intent on reaching and experimenting with more. It is unsurprising then, that the first entries in her personal dictionary tend to be everyday things that are dear to her and easy to say, such as "cat", "cup", "drink" and "ball". With objects, there is also the advantage that she can point to them to make her meaning clear.

All her own work

Of course, her speech production is by no means perfect yet, and her first words may only be intelligible to close family members. But they still qualify as words; the important point being that she is using sounds intentionally and consistently to tell you something.

When your baby discovers how well her words are received, she will enjoy the attention and repeat them often. Don't be impatient for more at this stage. She is learning that people like her to talk – that's a great start.

Checklist

Children pass these talking milestones in their second year:

- speech: they use strings of intonation and speech sounds that gradually become recognizable words
- expression: words appear slowly at first but, by two years, they may have about 200 words and be combining them into phrases and sentences
- comprehension: they understand more than they can say and will hand over familiar objects on request. They begin to understand verbs such as "run" and adjectives such as "little".

First words

These are the most common words that babies say first:

Objects
ball, book, car, chair, cup, dinner milk, shoe, spoon, sweet, teddy

People
Mummy, Daddy, other names

Actions
brush/comb, down, drink, eat, fall (down), go, gone/all gone, in, kiss, off, on, sit (down), sleep, stop, throw, up, want, wash

Pronouns
me, mine, I, you, it

Social
bye, gimme, hello/hi, night-night, here, look, no, yes, there, what, where

Adjectives
big, clean, dirty, hot, little, small, more, my, nice, sick, this, that, yours

Understanding more than she can say

Between the ages of one and two, children have a better understanding of life than they can express in words. They can usually respond to simple requests such as being asked to fetch shoes, and can extract words from conversation and anticipate routines. For example, your toddler may arrive in the hall with her big brother's bag when he is ready for school or head purposefully towards her highchair if you mention pasta for lunch.

Words are still a very new tool and can be frustrating when they fail to have the desired effect. Most of the time, your toddler falls back on expressive babbling, shrieks of pleasure, giggles and yells when she needs to get her message across.

Gestures such as raising her arms for a cuddle, pointing, kissing, clenching her fists and covering her eyes are still every bit as effective as words.

Building vocabulary

Toddlers learn to use about 10 new words and to understand as many as 20 new words each month during their second year. They will do this effortlessly if they are offered language-rich opportunities in the form of games, stories, one-to-one conversations and songs. Try some of the following ideas.

● Your child is actively listening for speech so be aware of background noise at home and check that there are quiet rooms in her care setting. Be sure she has plenty of one-to-one conversations with you or her carer.

GOOD LISTENER
Your toddler may not have many words of her own, but she will respond to simple requests such as "fetch your shoes" if you speak clearly and emphasize the important words.

• Keep her at the centre of occasions such as family meals when everyone is chatting freely, and translate her words and gestures for less familiar listeners so they can talk to her, too.

• Decide on a few words to work on, keep them in context and find lively ways to repeat them. If your first word is "apple", show her an apple and tell her what it is. Then try to bring it into your conversations: "Shall we give Tom an apple for his packed lunch?"; "I'm chopping up this apple for tea"; "Mmm, this apple is sweet." Point out apples in the supermarket and find pictures of them in books and magazines.

• Try hiding toys under a blanket or in a box and keep up a running commentary: "Ooh, teddy is running away"; "Look, teddy is hiding under a box". Say the words clearly, avoiding baby-talk variations such as "chuff-chuff" for train.

• Don't ask her to imitate words. She may be able to copy but it won't help her to use them herself.

First sentences

Once children have learned what a word is, it is not long before they are naming everything. Soon they progress to common actions, many of which start as nouns and then turn into verbs – for example, "brush", "bath" and "drink".

BODY TALK
Gestures make the meaning clear when she doesn't have enough words to say why she needs a cuddle right now.

When the pool of words is large enough, usually around 50 words, your child begins to combine two words to express more complex ideas. To begin with you may not be sure what these little sentences mean – "Luke doggy", for example, could mean "Luke's got a dog", or "That's Luke's dog" or "Luke is a dog"; you have to work it out from the context. But soon she starts using combinations of a subject with a verb such as "me dancing" or a verb with an object, "eat dinner". These have a much more precise meaning, even when they are out of context. Language is coming into its own.

Every man is "dad"

Words do not have built-in meanings and young children usually make slip-ups at first.

• Toddlers often overextend words, using them to cover things that have similar characteristics. For a while, all men may be called "daddies" and all four-legged animals may be called "dogs".

• They also underextend words, limiting their meaning to one item rather than lots of similar things. Early on, your toddler may insist that "buggy" refers only to her pushchair or that "cat" can only be the family cat.

My son's speech is hard to understand – should I correct him?

Children's speech becomes clearer the more they practise and the more they hear good examples of speech. For children under two, it is better if you simply model sentences correctly and encourage your child to listen rather than force him to say words properly. The meaning of what your child says to you is much more important than how correct it is.

At first you may find your child becomes harder to understand as he begins to say more. If his single words are unclear, they are likely to become more so when he starts to put them together. You need to be patient and attentive to stop him becoming frustrated and inhibited about expressing himself.

★ **Do** give him plenty of time to say what he has to say and give him your full attention. Let him know that you understand, and repeat it back to give him a clear example of how to say it.

★ **Do** help his listening by exaggerating your voice, saying LISTEN and pointing to your ear when you want to hold his attention.

★ **Do** read stories and sing songs and rhymes that draw his attention to listening to sounds.

★ **Don't** tell him he is wrong and ask him to say whatever he said again – he won't know what you are trying to get him to do.

★ **Don't** copy his speech or laugh at him.

★ **Don't** break up the words into individual sounds "m-i-l-k" and get him to copy them. This is unlikely to make much sense to a two year old.

★ **Don't** insist on correct grammar. At worst it causes frustration, at best hilarity, as in the case of the dad below trying to correct his son's speech.

Nathaniel: (pointing at head): Put back hat on.
Dad: No, you need to say "put my hat back on my head".
Nathaniel: Put hat on head.
Dad: No, repeat after me "put my hat"…
Nathaniel: Put my hat …
Dad: …back on…
Nathaniel: …back on…
Dad: …my head.
Nathaniel: …my head.
Dad: Let's put that together: "Put my hat back on my head".
Nathaniel: Put back hat on head.

Language opportunities

You don't need to organize elaborate outings for the under twos – taking a stroll round the garden or local park provides some great language opportunities, as long as you have time to make the most of them.

Quality time as far as language is concerned is best achieved with one-to-one exchanges about something of interest, and, for a toddler, the world has a limitless supply of fascinating things. Although there may be something you want to draw her attention to – a bee crawling into a flower or a worm disappearing into freshly turned earth – keep in mind the two-way nature of conversation and be ready to follow her lead, too. She may be more excited by simpler pleasures, so be prepared to chat to her about the joys of muddy puddles, too.

Some carers and parents get into the habit of delivering a moment-by-moment running commentary as a useful way to pass on words and information. Try not to overdo this or your child may begin to treat your voice as background noise and not pay much attention to it at all.

Expert tips

To get the best out of an outing:

● crouch down and follow her gaze so you can talk to her about the things she is interested in

● give her plenty of time – don't rush her on to the swings when she is still clearly enchanted by the antics of the ducks

● don't try to do too much – short trips are usually better than long ones.

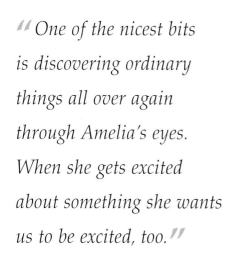

" One of the nicest bits is discovering ordinary things all over again through Amelia's eyes. When she gets excited about something she wants us to be excited, too. "

JOEL is dad to two-year-old Amelia

Follow his lead

Early talkers do better if people follow their lead in conversations. When you comment on what your child says, a link is made (experts call this "being contingent"), whereas if you make a different observation, your child may find it hard to follow you. This conversation between Declan and his mum starts to break down as soon as his mum changes subject.

Declan (aged 18 months): *Tain (train).*

Mum: *Yes it's a train going into the station.*

Declan: *Tain there*

Mum: *Yes, and can you see that lorry over there?*

Declan: *Big tain.*

Playing with words

Until school age and the years beyond, children learn mostly through play. Play is children's work; it is their route to making discoveries, exploring their surroundings safely and forming social relationships, and it takes all their energy and ingenuity.

Although there is little research that links adult involvement in play with language development, playing with your baby sends her the message that you are interested in what interests her. This is a boost to her confidence and will make her want to go on sharing experiences with you.

Just as it is helpful for children to have an adult speaker to show them how to interact, so it is useful for

PAT-A-CAKE
She loves rhymes with lots of noise and action and will soon be joining in, too. The hard part is bringing the game to an end.

them to have their parents join in games and provide new words for the toys and actions they are using. The trick is to know when to be involved and when to leave her to potter happily by herself.

You may find it is much easier to have relaxed conversations when you are doing something together, perhaps with bricks, farm animals, cars and garages, or dolls. Along the way, you will be giving your child examples of how to take turns, how to share and how to listen and act on another person's ideas. Although at this age she simply plays alongside rather than with her friends, she is gathering social skills that will help her to be a good playmate later on.

When you are choosing toys for this age group, keep in mind that young children don't need elaborate push-button toys that talk, flash and beep. These are enthralling at first, but once she knows which buttons to press, there is not much else to do. They also offer little impetus for anything but solitary play.

Rhymes and games

Toddlers like their games to be repetitive, so don't be too intense about finding variations to make play less predictable. Peekaboo and hiding games have enduring appeal, as have simple action rhymes with funny outcomes. She wrinkles her nose and squirms in anticipation of a tickle when you count "This little Piggy went to Market" on her toes or play "Round and Round the Garden" on the palm of her hand. Let her try to do it, too – she will love making her mummy shriek.

Soon she will be joining in the actions with songs such as "The Wheels on the Bus" and "Incey, Wincey Spider", humming to the tune and chiming in with feeling when there are words she can say – "spider", "up" and "down".

Questions & Answers

How can we help our active little daughter to pay attention and improve her ability to listen?

High levels of background noise make it difficult for young children to "tune in" to language, so make sure that the television and radio are turned off when no one is actively listening. Give her your full attention when she talks – it's quite possible to discourage children from listening by not listening to them.

Try games that focus her listening. "Sound lotto" uses a tape of different noises, such as a tap dripping and a plane taking off, and matching picture cards. You can buy one or make your own – try including the voices and photographs of your family members.

Our 20-month-old son knows what the word "no" means but now does the opposite whenever we say it. What shall we do?

Children of this age like to test out their limits and if "no" has become a game of wills with your son, perhaps you are overusing the word or applying it inconsistently and confusingly. If you reserve "no" for important safety issues or extreme behaviour, he will be more likely to take you seriously. Try organizing your home so that dangerous or vulnerable items are out of reach and avoid confrontations by distracting your son with other options. It is less frustrating for him and gets the same result as "no".

PUZZLE TALK
Doing puzzles together gives her pictures to discuss, and words for shape, size and fitting.

How does pretend play help my toddler to talk?

Your toddler would dearly love to take part in most of what adults do, but he is limited by his size and capability, the pressures on family time and the need to keep him safe. Pretend play allows him to be in control of a private world where he can test out his conversational skills and order events exactly how he pleases.

SIMPLE PROPS
Toddlers don't need elaborate toys – shoe boxes and a duster for a bed for teddy and a few small plastic cups and spoons are all he needs to get him started on pretend play.

Endless possibilities

A toddler under two is not yet ready to organize his own pretend play – at first, he needs help in setting a scene and someone to provide some simple props and demonstrate the possibilities:

★ Show him how to pretend to drink from a cup and then give some to you; put his teddy to bed in a shoe box; or use a bucket and sponge to wash his car. He will soon learn to copy and then start playing in this way by himself.

★ Early on he needs recognizable props, such as a realistic telephone or little cups and spoons, to get him started. Don't expect his games to last long or develop an interesting storyline at this age – he is too young to build ideas and will soon become bored if you make the game too elaborate.

★ It won't be long, however, before he begins to base his fantasies on almost anything that is available. A stick becomes his fishing rod; a pile of Lego, a pool; a banana, a telephone; a flat stone with daisies on it, dinner for his toys. While he is pretending, he is making judgements and plans and

SOCIAL GATHERINGS

Playing with a tea set and water gives him practice in fetching and carrying and pouring with no concerns about mess. He is also developing a range of social chatter as he offers drinks to siblings, playmates and parents, elicits pleases and thank yous and responds to requests for milk, sugar and biscuits.

ON THE PHONE

An old telephone or mobile phone is a wonderful language tool for a toddler. As he punctuates streams of sounds with "hello" and "goodbye", adopts a bored sing-song tone or shrieks with raucous laughter, you are are left in no doubt as to who he is mimicking.

picturing things in his mind as he would like them to be. These are the beginnings of real thinking.

★ During pretend play young children enter a safety zone where they can test out their fears and overcome their limitations. Your child is able to climb high, run fast, and dive and swim in his imagination. As he acts out his own feelings or mimics people around him, he is getting practice at controlling the order of events and displaying emotions – whether he is being consoling to a sick teddy or bossy with toys who won't go to bed.

Talking with books

Books are a great way of interacting with your young child. Being read to helps to focus her attention precisely on words because she has pictures to refer to while she is hearing them. She will also love the attention, cuddles and close contact that goes hand in hand with sharing a book.

● Just a few favourite books are all you need at first because toddlers enjoy repetition as much as novelty. They are proud of what they know and want to share it repeatedly. Choose books with realistic recognizable pictures that reflect your child's everyday experiences. She will enjoy joining in – lifting flaps to find hidden surprises and making animal noises in the right places.

● As a baby, your child may have simply pointed at the pictures, but now she is actively listening for words. Comment on what is happening on each page. Ask an occasional question – "What is the bear doing now?" – but not so many that it becomes a test; she will lose interest, especially if she is struggling to form words.

● By the age of two, children begin to enjoy books with a story and start to focus on sequences and cause and effect. Tell the story in your own words – it will bring it to life. The more children hear people modelling stories, the more they want to do it themselves.

Golden rules

Adults often feel that they have to be in control of children to show them what is what, but this can lead to very dull interaction with one party calling the shots and the other reacting. Spend time following the communication lead of your child. Begin by simply watching what she is doing; then venture a comment on some aspect of it: "You're putting the elephant in the truck now." Try to expand on her reply to extend her vocabulary and understanding. "The elephant's very big isn't he… is he going to fit, do you think?" Don't try to distract your child away from the focus of her attention – go with it.

It's very easy for adults to anticipate a toddler's interests and needs and supply all the dialogue without her having to say much at all. She responds with a nod or shake of the head while you chatter on relentlessly. Make it a habit to listen carefully to your toddler and be patient if you don't understand at first. Think of the effort she is putting into these first statements and value them accordingly.

When she gets things wrong it's because she has limited words at her disposal and so is using what she has to elicit more information. Give her the correct word in a positive way rather than starting with a "no".

Avoiding baby talk

Perhaps one of the most important messages of this book is that you should be natural with your child. Although the parentese style of talk (see page 20) helps babies to focus on language, some parents feel they need to go further and use a special vocabulary, too. Dogs become "bow wows"; cats are "kitty-cats"; trains are "chuff-chuffs" and cars are "broom-brooms". Babytalk like this is of no particular value, and must at times be puzzling for a child, particularly if she spends time in settings where everyone uses the proper words.

The only really useful baby words are your child's own – her first attempts at words based on what she can manage to say. For a while a cushion may be a "pushun" because she can't quite produce a /k/ sound, or a fish, a "dit" until she can say /f/ and /sh/. However adorable you find these early versions of words, be happy to relinquish them as soon as she does. She shouldn't be made to feel that her baby pronunciation is so cute it is something that she needs to hold on to.

GOOD LISTENERS
Friends who listen with interest teach your toddler that her talk is important.

Expert tips

Try these 10 tips for keeping the conversation going.

- Actively engage in your child's earliest communication.
- Listen carefully and value what she has to say.
- Follow her communication lead.
- Expand on what she says.
- Show that you are interested in what she has to say and that it is important to you.
- Be natural – don't use "baby language" or try to "teach" her how to speak.
- Engage in her play.
- Tell stories that she can understand.
- Give her confidence to keep on communicating.
- Help her speak to other people by translating the words she says that are hard to understand.

" Euan has developed such an **imagination.** He likes nothing better than to invent games and **make up his own stories**. It wins him a lot of friends. **"**

MARGARET is mum to six-year-old Euan

4

A language explosion

By two years of age children are gathering words, putting them together and finding they can say any number of complicated things. Over the next three years, language develops extraordinarily fast, and parents are often amazed by the breadth and sophistication of the things their children can now say.

Adding to the dictionary

By the start of their second year, many children have more than 200 words at their disposal. By the time they are six, experts have stopped counting, but a vocabulary of 15,000 words is not unusual. During a child's third year, there is a vocabulary burst in which children seem to add to their dictionary of words on almost a daily basis. This is followed by a grammar burst when they start to use all their language tools together to, for example, speak sentences with a past and future and use pronouns, such as "me" and "you".

No longer babies, two to three-year-old children push continually at the boundaries to make discoveries. Their on-button seems to be switched on permanently; they have good control of their bodies and limbs and are limited only by lack of experience and their parents' need to keep them safe and to some sort of schedule.

Your child is still learning through his senses and will love to mess with sand and water, smell flowers, whirl around to music, and test himself on a climbing frame, but language is now an essential part of his discoveries. He needs a constant supply of names of things so he can talk about what engages him as well as answers to "what", "why" and "how".

Fuelling the train

At first, language springs from his interests and activities, but soon it is feeding into and enriching them enabling him to describe, relate, explain, argue, question and fantasize. At times it may seem as if your child's talking has become a runaway train that needs little help to keep it going. Not at all – you fuel his progress by offering new vocabulary, experiences and examples of good speech, and stoke him up with confidence in his talking.

Checklist

2–3 years: speaks two to three-word sentences and can find familiar objects on request. Produces a good range of sounds.

3–4 years: talks increasingly fluently. Can refer to past and future events. Understands concepts such as colour and size and most of what parents say to him.

4–5 years: speech is completely intelligible except for occasional errors. Uses questions. Can understand and retell a story from a book or tell one of his own. Understands abstract words such as "always".

Tackling grammar

One of the more complex aspects of language is the way words change to create different meanings. In English grammar, for example, adding an "s" to most words makes a plural (so "cat" becomes "cats"), but, confusingly, adding "s" also indicates possession (as in the "cat's whiskers"). And of course there are exceptions to the rules: "mouse" changes to "mice" in the plural. And what about the past tense?

Most of the time adding "ed" to a word does the trick –"The princess danced beautifully". But some verbs like "go" change in the past tense – "The princess went (not goed) home afterwards." When children learn a second language at school they have pages of rules and irregular verbs and plurals to learn, yet babies and young children grasp the complexities of their first language entirely by listening to speech and using it.

Interestingly, one of the clues that your child is engaging with grammar is when he begins to make slip-ups, sometimes with sentences he used to say accurately. Before the age of two he might say "Dog sat down" or "See mice", only to switch later to "I sitted down" or "Look at all the mouses". Now that he is applying grammar to what he says, rather than parroting little phrases, he has to sort out which words don't follow the rules.

Temper tantrums

Two to three-year-olds often feel overwhelmed by the sheer unmanageability of events, and often the result is a temper tantrum. When one occurs, your usually amenable little girl is transformed into a screaming, kicking, breath-holding dervish. Although you find tantrums upsetting, her rage is frightening to her, too. It is as if all her newly acquired skills of communication have deserted her.

● Although tantrums are usually focused on something forbidden, they tend to occur when a child is tired, hungry, bored or temporarily overlooked. Are you ignoring her? Have you been shopping for hours and trying not to notice her whining about it? Stop and take a break.

● When you sense a tantrum may be in the offing, offer her a way out that gives her some control over events – "You pick a table and we'll sit down and have a drink." Be prompt, because rewarding her during or after the tantrum sends out the wrong message.

● If she is beyond reason, don't join in and scream and shout, too. Take her to somewhere safe, stay close and leave her to work through her mood.

● Afterwards, cuddle your child and reassure her that, although you don't much like her tantrums, you still love her. At times when she is behaving well, make a point of noticing and rewarding her good behaviour.

You don't need to correct your child's mistakes, just reflect back to him what he said using the correct words. When he says "Mum, we slept in the tent in the garden", you reply along the lines of "My goodness, you slept in the tent! Was it very cold and wet?"

Language gets complicated

A toddler's first sentences, such as "Daddy gone" and "Eat dinner", are rather remarkable because they are almost always grammatically correct. As children become competent talkers, they not only use more complicated arrangements of words to make sentences but also begin to string ideas together. Conjunctions such as "and" and "but" do the job at first, but they soon progress to "so" and "because", although these are often used interchangeably at first, as in – "He sat on my bike because it's broken" and "I chose this dress so it's pink."

Time words are tricky, too, because young children do not have enough experience to unpick the meaning of "weeks", "months" and "years". Even a day is best described as a series of events from breakfast to bedtime.

Pronouns can also be a problem: your son knows his name early on but at different times he has to sort out whether he is "I", "me" or "mine".

Most children are fluent talkers by the age of six, but semantic development continues through junior school and beyond as they tackle increasingly complex sentences using, for example, the conditional tense – "If I had a hamster, I would clean its cage" – and the passive voice – "The fish was eaten by a bear".

Expert tips

"Simon says" is a good way to boost your child's comprehension as well as pass on vocabulary.

● Take it in turns to give orders such as "Simon says – touch your toes".

● Make the requests more complicated as your child gets faster at reacting but keep the game uncompetitive for young children or for a mix of ages.

Fluent at four

Most children are fluent talkers at four. This is Carl talking to his mum about a Spider-man® video:

Carl: *There was a big party and suddenly they were being attacked… and Spider-man jumped down the side of the building and fighted with Green Goblin.*

Mum: *And what happened then?*

Carl: *I dunno. Green Goblin made these rocket things came out and they hit Spider-man and he fell down. But he got up and caught Green Goblin in his web.*

Mum: *It sounds a bit frightening.*

Carl: *No, not really.*

Mum: *What did you do when they were fighting?*

Carl: *Well, I hid my face. It was a bit scary…*

Carl can string several simple sentences together to tell a story and also describe how he felt when he was watching his video. The only mistake he makes is when he adds "–ed" to "fight" to make "fighted" instead of "fought".

SHARING AND SWAPPING
Learning to keep everyone happy is an important part of play between older and younger children.

Playing and talking

Pre-school children learn a great deal by copying and, given the right-sized equipment and careful demonstrations, become more than capable of tasks such as dressing themselves or pouring out drinks.

They enjoy playing "as if" games that involve using a different voice and facial expressions to become someone else, just as they like to try on grown-ups' shoes and hats to see what it is like to be big.

As your child gets older, you may feel there is less of a need to join in his play, but he still appreciates your interest even if you don't always take an active role in the game. As always, follow your child. At best,

you can boost the language possibilities of a shopping game with lots of new names of food and fruit as well as putting some hilarious items on sale. At worst, you can take it upon yourself to teach everyone to give change accurately.

Games that span the ages

Young children like nothing better than to watch and copy what their older brothers and sisters do, as well as to be able to talk to them and engage with them. A young child can learn a great deal about the practical aspects of communication from older children's play, as well as find the idiosyncratic nature of it stimulating and exciting. Older children also benefit from the experience of organizing and scaling down activities, negotiating over toys and having to take a younger person's abilities into account. Even a pre-school child, it seems, is able to automatically adjust his speech to the right level for a younger toddler.

There are lots of games and activities that span a broad age range and make it possible for everyone to take part. Table-top games work well; choose the sort that are easy to set up and are not too complicated. It's probably better to play the same game several times at first so everyone becomes familiar with it. Picture lotto is a game that can be played with children of all ages down to 18 months. Not only is picture matching a useful visual activity, the pictures provide good opportunities for talk.

Great days out

Almost any outing from an afternoon at the market to a full-scale day out on the beach is an opportunity to get your child commenting on what he is seeing and experiencing. Home in on the things he finds interesting and try to extend his experiences. If you can take back some memory prompts, a selection of exotic fruit from a stall to taste with the rest of the family or some shells and postcards, they can be a focus for talking about what you did together.

Photographs are a great way to stimulate language because children

Expert tips

Try these tips on days out with pre-school and older children.

● Be attentive to your child. Don't assume he will pick up all he needs while you chat to a friend.

● Follow your child's lead rather than deliver lectures on aspects that seem most educational.

● Don't ask too many questions. If you quiz him all the time he may get tired of responding.

● A four year old who likes dinosaurs can usually tackle quite complicated names, such as Tyrannosaurus Rex, so don't be scared off by unusual names of, for example, animals at the zoo. Once he has a good smattering of common names, tell him about the gnus and Przewalski horses, too.

PLAYING GAMES
Learning to take turns, settle disputes and win or lose with good grace makes everyone a winner socially.

Is TV bad for pre-school children?

Television isn't bad for pre-school children but it is often misused. Managed well, TV delights and entertains and extends their interest in the world. Used badly, TV is a babysitter who does not let them speak. Parked in front of the TV for hours on end, your pre-schooler absorbs very little and wastes the opportunity to do so much more.

Television and talking

If you sat your baby in front of the television all day every day, he would not learn to talk. To learn language effectively, he needs responsive partners who listen to what he says, answer him and show him that what he has to say is important. Even the most engaging of television programmes cannot be responsive in this way, nor can so-called interactive television and computer games.

★ To small babies, TV is just non-stop noise and may have the negative effect of preventing them learning to listen to language or anything else.

★ Before the age of two, children don't need television at all. Usually, they don't find it particularly interesting because they cannot make sense of the stream of images, but high levels of background noise from the TV affects their ability to concentrate. It is often distracting enough to prevent them doing more interesting things.

★ The best way to use TV with an older child is to spend time watching with him so TV becomes a shared experience like a book. You can then talk together about what you have seen and heard and and sort out anything he does not understand.

WATCHING TOGETHER
The best way to use television is to treat it like a book. Adopt the habit of chatting about what you are seeing on the screen and relating it to other things that he knows about.

★ Restricting TV to watching favourite videos is easier to control than trying to pick from a constant flow of children's programmes on all channels. Familiar videos are an ideal way of encouraging your child to speak about what he has seen and sing or gesture along with familiar songs.

★ As he gets older, establish a fixed quota of TV each day or week and encourage him to be selective. It will help him develop good judgement.

love to see themselves in a setting and talk about what they remember doing at the beach or in the park.

Keeping it simple

Offering simple choices between two T-shirts or a drink of juice or milk helps young children feel in control and involved in decisions. However, broad choices can leave them confused and upset – they may not have enough information to pick from a tray of cakes or a rack of dresses. Even harder is being asked to make choices between, for example, staying in the car with dad or going to the shops with mum. Your child can't imagine what the two options entail nor hold them in mind to compare them. Whatever he chooses feels like the wrong choice.

Too young to deceive

Trying to extract promises from a child under three is also a problem because he cannot comprehend the extra meaning that makes "promising" different from simply "saying". To make a promise, and also to tell a lie, he has to be able to form an idea of what someone else wants to happen, and he doesn't yet have this insight into other people's point of view.

Between the age of three and five, children begin to reflect on what they know and on what they need

TELL IT LIKE IT IS
Skipping a few pages because you are in a rush is no longer an option. She knows how the story should go.

to tell other people to achieve a particular end. This is the stage when they become capable of telling a lie. Try this test to see if your child has insight into another point of view:

"A little boy hides a packet of sweets in a wooden box in his bedroom. He goes to have lunch. While he is out of the room, his sister takes out the sweets and puts them under the bed. When the little boy comes back into the bedroom, where will he look for the sweets?"

If your son says "under the bed" he is still basing his answers on what he himself knows. If he answers "in the box", it shows he is now able to think through what the boy in the story knows (and does not know) about the whereabouts of his sweets.

Sticking to the story

You may find your pre-schooler is much fussier about his stories than he was previously. Innovation is out: he likes them told in exactly the same way each time. He may do a convincing imitation of reading alone, turning the pages and remembering and repeating whole sentences aloud. He's making a great start at becoming a reader.

Questions & Answers

My little girl was a very early talker but her younger brother has only a few sentences at two. Why are they so different?
It's common for boys (although not all boys) to be a little slower than girls in their language development, and if your daughter was an early talker, the difference may be more noticeable. Does your daughter talk for your son, or does her chatter draw most of your attention? Another factor may be your busy schedule with two children, in which case your son may just need more one-to-one conversation. If you're still worried after a few months, seek professional advice.

Expert tips

If your child is at the age when his questions never seem to stop, try the following advice.

- Offer a simple answer first. If he asks why an egg has a yellow middle you may not need to embark on the life cycle of chickens. He may be content to know that this bit is called the yolk, and this bit the white.

- Be honest when you don't know. Offer to help him find out in a book later on, if necessary.

- Don't be sarcastic or make up silly answers – he won't understand.

- If the questions are becoming a game, he may just want attention. Offer to do something together.

- Ask him what he thinks the answer is. He may have a good idea himself.

"I can cope with her questions about the moon and stars – but I dread her small but piping voice asking why that man has a big, red nose."

EVA is mum to three-year-old Sophie

Why he asks why

Somewhere between the age of two and three, children learn to ask questions. Initially they ask "what that?" and "who's that?" – the sort of questions that are much easier for parents to answer than the one that comes along next – "why?" Why represents a clear shift in the balance of power between the parent and the child and adults often feel as if they have been put on the back foot having to explain why they are going to do something or why something works in the way that it does. For a child, "why" is the perfect tool for finding out about things and making an adult respond to them.

Creating opportunities where questions are raised and answered incidentally can take off the pressure when "why" is the word that is constantly on your child's lips.

Joint projects such as cooking offer relaxed opportunities for talking about what you are doing, suggesting how to do something, and explaining why. Allow plenty of time so your child can make choices about details such as ingredients and decorations. The trick is to avoid marshalling him through a set of stages or taking over a task because he is not fast enough.

If you are short of time, remember that grandparents can be in a league of their own when it comes to easy exchanges of information while they are pottering in the garden with a grandchild or mending something.

Finding out together

Children's questions provide a wonderful opportunity to share what you know, so try not to fall back on "because that's the way it is", even if you are tired or under pressure. Often your child is just making a casual inquiry for a little bit more information and needs only a simple answer. However, if you get locked into a string of whys, it might be easier simply to talk to him about what he is interested in and see if you cover the ground. If you don't know the answer, be honest about it and make a note to look it up together later in a children's reference book or on a suitable internet site.

SHARED KNOWLEDGE
Grandparents with time to spare are often happy to pass on what they know and give their grandchild some safe hands-on experience.

Questions & Answers

My son is enchanted with naughty words. How can I stop him saying "poo-poo" to all and sundry?
Naughty words are not naughty in themselves; they are just being said at the wrong time. Words such as "poo-poo" and "wee-wee" are common currency during potty training but gain a certain power when children realize they can get a reaction by saying them.

So don't overact. Mild boredom is the best response until he is old enough for you to explain that what is appropriate amongst his friends doesn't go down so well with Grandma.

Often, it's just the sound of the words that appeals. Try responding with an alternative "naughty" word that sounds just as cheeky, such as "ping pong". He may get attached to that instead.

COUNTING AND SHARING
The best lessons in learning to count are when everyone cares about the outcome. Children enjoy sharing out treats so everyone gets a fair share.

Kind words

Look for ways to help your child empathize with friends and family members. It will give him insight into how other people think, and stand him in good stead later on.

● "Emma's fallen over – let's go and make sure she's all right. Help me find a plaster for her knee."

● "Josh is sad because his truck got broken. Let's see if we can find a way to cheer him up."

● "Mummy will be very tired when she gets home from work. Shall we make supper to give her a big surprise?"

In the wider world

When children start nursery and school, language and communication skills become increasingly important. Language is not just a way of capturing thoughts or telling mum what happened – it becomes the means through which they interact with their teacher, make and keep friends, negotiate disputes and access the school curriculum.

Over the next few years, teachers and parents begin to place much more emphasis on children's ability to develop literacy and numeracy skills, but it's worth remembering that these important skills are built entirely upon early language skills. To be able to read, children need to be able to know about language,

to sound out the different parts of words and then put them together again. Likewise they need to be able to make sense of what they read.

People sometimes think that number work is simply about calculation, but your child needs to be able to understand instructions to be able to work through problems. Without language this is almost impossible.

Like many parents, you may feel more removed from your child's daily life once he starts nursery or school, and at one level this is probably true. Remember, though, that your child carries with him the assumption of your interest in everything he does as well as all his early positive experiences of communication and learning to talk.

How can I help my shy child?

Some children don't have a burning desire to communicate, or they may actively avoid it. Shy children don't necessarily have any particular difficulty with listening to or understanding what is said to them, and their speech may be perfectly clear – they just seem to find the whole process of communication difficult.

Why is she shy?

Many children are shy and find social interaction difficult. Often it is simply because they are reluctant to communicate with people they don't know well. A child who, for example, has a close-knit family life until she starts nursery or school may not have the same confidence as another who has been in daycare from an early age. You can help by giving your child plenty of practice in talking to family members and using some of the following tips.

★ Build her self-esteem. Praise and encourage her, especially when she is trying something new, acting independently or playing sociably with a friend.

★ If she finds it difficult to manage new situations, give her plenty of preparation by reading books about children in similar circumstances.

★ Don't get into the habit of speaking for your child. Encourage her to ask for things herself in shops. Act as an interpreter if she finds other people hard to understand. Don't tell everyone that "she's just shy" – it reinforces the idea.

★ If your child has realized that she can have a considerable effect on others by not speaking, try not to overreact or become exasperated.

CLINGY CHILD
In new situations, let her stay close to you until she begins to feel comfortable. Ease her path into a new group of children by joining her for a short time and making introductions.

" I didn't know what to **expect** of Abi's language development. We were both working and didn't have much contact with other children so we didn't really compare her with **anyone else.** "

ESTHER is mum to seven-year-old Abi

5

Checking on progress

Some children take longer to learn to talk than others and, although parents may worry about a slight delay, it does not necessarily mean that language is going to be a problem in the future. Keeping a careful check on your child's progress will help you decide if and when you need to get to help.

Making comparisons

Speech and language development is such an obvious part of a child's growing up it is one of the most common areas in which parents seek reassurance. Knowing what to expect can be difficult, however, if you have little experience of children other than your own, and if you do make comparisons with other children, you are likely to focus on the most proficient talkers rather than the range of accomplishments across your child's age group. Your own parents may also make comparisons across the generations that cannot always be relied upon.

Like adults, children find some activities easier than others, and although their development tends to follow the same sequence, the exact age at which skills develop differs from one child to the next. In this respect, language learning is no different from any other aspect of a child's development. Each new skill develops within a broad period; whether your child masters it early or late within the timespan, she can still be considered to be developing normally. The previous chapters and checklists in this book should give you a feel for how your child's language skills are progressing, while the checklist on page 59 highlights some key signs of a speech or language delay.

More than speech

Many children continue to make minor errors with their speech at the age of four and some will go on having problems with the pronunciation of more difficult sounds for several years. So when you are considering your child's progress it's important that you look beyond speech and also focus on the language that she understands and how she expresses herself.

Checklist

Some reasons why children may have difficulties learning to communicate:

- problems associated with being born very prematurely or born severely underweight
- general or specific language difficulties, which may be inherited
- high levels of stress in the family or at nursery or school
- sensory impairment – hearing and/or visual difficulties
- a problem such as dyspraxia or dyslexia
- autistic spectrum disorder
- being a twin.

Bilingual children

Bilingual children learn to talk in the same way as other children, although they may be a little slower when they start because they are learning words across languages. Most bilingual children catch up quickly, and parents need to assess how many words their child has in both languages to decide whether there is a problem or not.

● If you and your partner speak different languages, stick to your own first language with your child. When your child starts nursery the language she is immersed in becomes dominant. Although her second language may not become as sophisticated as her first, the facility to speak it will stay with her.

● You need to be consistent to keep her second language active. Sing nursery rhymes and read stories to her in her second language for as long as she allows it. Keep close contact with grandparents and family members.

● Encourage her to be proud of her skill. Bilingual children are thought to be more aware of language and this may help other learning in school.

● Trying to teach a baby a language that is not your own is usually a waste of energy and may confuse and discourage her during an important learning period. Unless you are fluent, you are likely to pass on a faulty accent and errors. If you are fluent, wait until she is at least five years old, and fully competent in her own language.

Checklist

Some sounds are more difficult to say than others and children may not master these until they are about eight. These are the ages by which about 90 per cent of children are able to say the following sounds:

● by 3 years: p, m, h, n, w

● by 4 years: b, k, g, d, f, y

● by 6 years: t, r, l

● by 7 years: z

● by 8 years: s, v, th

Listening and attention

How well does your child attend to what is going on around her by looking and listening? Being able to control and decide what needs her attention most at particular times is essential to language and to much of her later learning. There may be a variety of reasons why she does not respond as she should; for example, her ability to hear is crucial (see page 57). A home with constant loud background noise does not help her listening skills, and there are other family dynamics (see page 61) that may make her switch off attention. What you need to be sure of is that she is able to listen if she wants to.

Verbal understanding

Children know what to expect of the daily round of mealtimes, trips to nursery and bedtimes so it may not be clear how much they understand from the language associated with these routines. Verbal understanding is your child's ability to extract information from the language she hears, regardless of the context. Try the comprehension tests in the box on the right to see how much she understands from language alone.

Vocabulary, language and speech

After the age of two, vocabulary expands dramatically and then seems to kick-start grammar activity as children put words together to make sentences. If your child has been struggling with language, she may reach this point later than others.

One sign of this is that she continues to use gestures more than words after the age of two.

By the age of four, your child should be talking fluently, using a range of tenses, and stringing clauses together to make complicated sentences. Try asking her to retell a favourite story to see how well she is able to sequence information.

By six, her speech is comparable with an adult's, although she may still have difficulty pronouncing some sounds such as /th/ and /r/.

> **TELL ME ABOUT IT**
> *Asking your child what he likes about a favourite toy is a good way of finding out how well he can express himself.*

> ### Expert tips
>
> **These ideas help to test your child's verbal understanding.**
>
> ● **2–3 years** Get a small suitcase and ask your child to help you pack. Ask him to bring his shoes, socks, pants, coat, etc.
>
> ● **3–4 years** Ask your child to act out instructions using toys. Include a mix of words such as "fast and slow", "under and over", "in and out". For example, "Now your spider crawls under the pillow…"
>
> ● **4–5 years** Show pictures of animals and household objects and pose questions: "Which animals climb trees?"; "What do we use when we want to cook bacon and eggs?"

Expert tips

If your child is 18 months to two years old, try this test to check how well she coordinates her lips and tongue – a necessary skill for speaking words. Give her a dry, crumbly biscuit and watch how she eats it.

• Does she bite off small bits and deal with each in turn or does she stuff the whole thing into her mouth?

• Does she leave crumbs around her mouth or is she able to coordinate her lips and tongue to lick them off?

• If she misses some crumbs on her face and you draw her attention to them, can she then lick them off?

Some children do not manage to pronounce these sounds correctly until around the age of eight.

A lisp is often caused by a tooth problem because, to produce a clear /s/ sound, a child needs to be able to expel air through a tiny gap between her teeth. Gappy or missing teeth can make pronunciation difficult as can wearing orthodontic braces later on. Most children manage these trickier sounds eventually as they develop the muscles they need for speech, but if problems persist, a speech therapist can show your child how to position her tongue and lips while she practises the sounds.

Looking at the whole child

Speech is often a focus for parents' concern but it is important to look at all aspects of a child's development because difficulties often occur together. General learning difficulties are the most common source of speech and language difficulties. A child who is slow to start doing all sorts of things, such as crawling, walking and feeding herself is likely to develop language and speech slowly, too. Depending on the severity of a child's difficulties, this need not be a problem as long as her parents and teachers are aware of her needs and make sure she has support.

CHECKING DEVELOPMENT
Use your child's regular developmental checks to talk through concerns with your GP or health visitor.

A language problem

Some children, however, have trouble acquiring language even though all their other learning skills are intact. Primary language difficulties (or specific language difficulties) are thought to run in families. Sometimes the problem is that a child simply cannot understand what others are saying. This may be hard to pick up at first because young children often get by using context and visual cues.

In other cases, children understand what people say but are unable to form sentences at the right level for their age and so carry on using gestures rather than speech. They can become very frustrated as they struggle to get their meaning across. Later on, they find it difficult to, for example, form past and future tenses, or organize their ideas into stories. They may also go on to have difficulties learning to read and write.

A speech difficulty

Most children's speech is difficult to understand at times, but those with a specific speech difficulty cannot communicate because they either use too few speech sounds or continue to use the sounds they developed as babies. They know what they want to say but are frustrated because they cannot access the right sounds.

MULTIPLE SKILLS
He needs language and fine motor skills to pick up a pencil and write down his thoughts.

Questions & Answers

My four-year-old son is beginning to stammer. Does he need to have speech therapy?
Most children stammer occasionally, especially when they are excited and their ideas outstrip their vocabulary. You can help your son by trying not to finish words for him or being impatient or embarrassed when he speaks and not forcing him to speak when he is nervous. The checklist below will help you decide if your child has a difficulty that is becoming entrenched. If you are concerned, ask for him to be referred for speech and language therapy.

• Does he talk normally when he is on his own or with close friends and family? Stammering may simply be due to anxiety about talking to strangers.

• Is he frustrated by his speech and becoming aware that he has a problem? If so, seek professional advice.

• Does he repeat words or parts of words or show tension and "block" when he starts to speak? Sounds at the beginning of words are often a problem for children who stammer.

How can we make sure our twin girls develop speech normally?
Twins are often late talkers, partly because they are usually premature or low birthweight babies but also because their parents may have less time for individual language activities than parents of single children. It's not uncommon for twins to develop their own language or "idioglossia" understood only by each other.

To avoid problems, try to find opportunities for your twins to speak and act individually. Arrange separate outings, and encourage turn-taking in your conversations with them both. Be careful to direct your questions and answers to just one child at a time.

Autistic children

Children with autistic spectrum disorders have problems with communication, social interaction and behaviour that affect their ability to form relationships with people. These complex disorders usually appear in the first three years of life.

• A baby with autism may be hard to console and unresponsive to the usual smiles and gestures.

• Autistic children seem to lack the desire to interact with others, particularly other children.

• If speech develops, it is used in a very concrete way, for example, only to express needs. Autistic children often repeat words and phrases, use them inappropriately or simply echo back what they hear. Language is taken literally and verbal jokes, inferences and figures of speech, such as "I could eat a horse", are confusing and even upsetting to them. They also find it difficult to read the body language, facial expressions, reactions and emotions of other people.

• One of the most common traits of autism is repetitive behaviour such as tapping, rocking, head–banging and teeth grinding. Later on, a child may be obsessed with arranging objects in a particular way or with a particular topic of conversation. Most autistic children are very resistant to changes in routine.

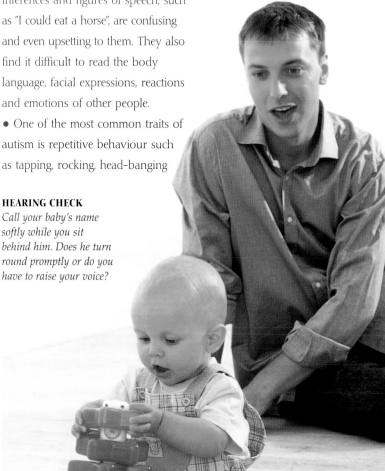

HEARING CHECK
Call your baby's name softly while you sit behind him. Does he turn round promptly or do you have to raise your voice?

Checklist

On a day-to-day basis, the best person to monitor your child's hearing is you. Use the checklist on page 17 during her first year, then continue to watch for signs that she may not be hearing well.

• Is she unresponsive or badly behaved after a cold or ear infection?

• Does she fail to react when called?

• Does she appear inattentive? Is she prone to daydreaming?

• Is she unsettled at nursery or school?

• Does she put the TV on too loud?

• Does she talk loudly?

• Does she mispronounce words?

• Is she often grumpy, frustrated and overactive?

Hearing difficulties

Although your child's ability to hear is critical to her learning to speak, there is much that can be done for children with reduced or absent hearing in terms of developing sign language and lip reading skills. Non-hearing children develop language skills at the same speed as hearing children if they are diagnosed early on. This is why hearing is tested at birth in the US, with a similar programme being introduced in the UK (see Hearing tests, below).

Over the next few years, your child will have further tests to check on conductive hearing loss. This is often due to glue ear – a build up of thick fluid behind the eardrum following repeated colds and ear infections.

Treatment varies, but children are sometimes fitted with grommets – tiny tubes that are inserted in the eardrum to release fluid and restore hearing to normal.

A child can also have hearing difficulties due to a build-up of ear wax inside the ear. This is a common minor disorder that is usually solved with ear drops or syringing.

Hearing tests

• First hearing test
A new NHS screening test, called the otoacoustic emission test, is being introduced nationwide to detect babies who are born with a sensori-neural problem that affects their hearing. For the test, a baby wears earpieces attached to a computer and a click is sent to the ear. If the ear returns an echo, hearing is normal. If no echo is detected, the baby has a second test called the auditory brain stem response. Small sensors are attached to her head, and clicking noises are played to the ears through headphones. A computer measures the auditory response within her brain.

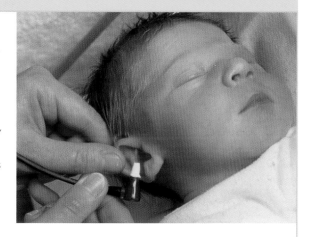

• Distraction test
The next test, called the distraction test usually takes place at about seven months. One assessor distracts your child with a toy, then hides it briefly. At this point another assessor, who is standing behind your child, shakes a light rattle or object that makes a soft sound. If your child turns to the sound automatically, she is hearing normally. However, there is a wide margin of error with this test, especially in slightly older babies who become so totally absorbed in finding the toy that has been hidden it is unclear whether they are hearing the rattle or not.

• Speech discrimination test
In this test, which takes place when a baby is about 18 months old, your child sits with a row of toys facing her, the names of which include sounds that cover the full range of hearing frequencies. The tester first makes sure your child can identify and knows the name for each item and then covers her own mouth and whispers the words very softly to see if your child is able to hear them and point to the correct toy.

• Pure tone audiometry
Your child may be offered a specialized hearing test called pure tone audiometry if a hearing problem is suspected. It is not usually given to children under four because they are unlikely to be mature enough to tolerate wearing headphones. Sounds of different volumes and frequencies are played through the headphones, and your child has to drop a brick into a box whenever she hears a sound.

When should I be concerned?

Deciding exactly when your child has reached a point in her language development when she needs help is not always easy. Consider some of the following ideas if you are worried about any aspect of her language and speech. If you are still concerned, see your doctor or health visitor, who will be able to refer her for expert assessment.

WATCH AND LISTEN
Spending time observing and listening to your child when she is alone with you or with her friends will help you decide if she needs to have some help with her communication.

Things to consider

★ Make time for your child to have relaxed conversations with you. If she has older siblings, she may not have had quite the same attention as your first child. Does she have an older brother or sister who does the talking for her?

★ Make sure her care arrangements have sufficient staff for plenty of one-to-one interaction. Avoid using an au pair or helper who does not speak much English – your child will be missing out on early language opportunities.

★ If possible, video your child at regular intervals and note any behaviour that strikes you as unusual. Ask people in regular contact with your child, such as her nursery teacher, how she seems in comparison to the rest of her group.

★ Tune in to what she is trying to say rather than trying to teach her specific things. You can then extend her interest by adding new information. Involving other children or older brothers and sisters in language games makes them less intense.

★ Use the checklist opposite to decide whether your child appears to have a specific language weakness that needs diagnosis and therapy.

Not always bad behaviour

Most children go through stages in their early years when they are hard to control. The "terrible twos" (the period between two and three years of age) is often a time when children begin to assert themselves to show off their new-found independence as well as their physical and language skills. This is also the time when parents learn to adapt their style of management to one that is more reasoned and negotiable. Although this period tests us as parents, it is a perfectly normal phase which most children go through.

Some children, however, remain difficult to manage in nursery and through into their primary school. When this happens it is important to think carefully about what might be causing this "naughty" behaviour. Is your child being rebellious and wilful or has she not understood what is expected of her?

Watch carefully to see what leads up to the episodes of naughtiness. If you know your child has problems with attention, make sure she is looking at you and listening when you tell her what you want her to do. If she finds it hard to understand a string of instructions, you or her carer or teacher need to issue them individually and make sure she understands each one in turn.

BREAKING POINT
When children's skills of negotiation break down it may end in a fight. Some adults are not so very different!

Checklist

Potential areas of concern in language development:

0–1 years: baby does not coo or babble; little or no communication

1–2 years: little variation in sounds; no meaningful intonation; no words by 18 months; no recognition of words for familiar objects; little attempt to communicate

2–3 years: understands little of what is said; restricted vocabulary; no word combinations; unable to find two items on request by two and a half.

3–4 years: much of what is said is unintelligible; says little or continues to echo what is said; restricted use of verbs/adjectives; comprehension outside everyday context very limited

4–5 years: speech largely unintelligible; uses single words or very simple grammar; little idea of tense; unable to retell a story; cannot cope in unfamiliar settings; increasing frustration and isolation.

Ready to read

Once your child has learned the basics of language, he begins to be able to talk about language and demonstrate what he knows. These skills, known as "metalinguistic" abilities, are the basis of many verbal games and also key to the development of his literacy skills. At their simplest level they include understanding that "cat" and "cup" begin with same sound, or recognizing alliteration (when words start with the same sounds – Peter Piper picked a peck of pickled peppers), or enjoying playing games with rhymes. These skills are a sign that your child is ready to get to grips with reading.

Keep up the conversation

Although you may feel there is not much left to think about once you are confident that your child's language is progressing normally, your conversational style continues to have an effect right through her childhood and teenage years. We all try to avoid people who talk only about their own problems, ask questions and don't listen to the answers or bark out orders without taking other points of view into account, but most parents do this, at least occasionally. If you feel your family is getting stuck in a conversational rut, try some strategies to get back on a firmer footing.

● Do you ask your child the same questions every day: "How was school?" or "What did you do at nursery?" Most days follow a similar pattern and her answer is usually "nothing" because nothing springs to mind. Try asking what was the best thing that happened today or the worst – it gives her something to focus her thoughts on.

● She hands you her model or painting and you say "that's lovely" and stick it on the fridge. In less than a minute you could have asked her how she made it, why she likes big green splodges, what the springy thing on the top is for and who else made what.

● Do all your questions get answered with "yes" or "no"? Reframe them to make them open ended. Instead of "Can you see those geese in the sky", try asking – "Where do you think those geese are going?"

• Tell her a small detail from your working day so she can imagine what you do in the hours you are away from her. Take her to see your work when you have a chance.

• Laugh at her jokes and listen to what she loves about Barbie or her favourite cartoon. Being an adult doesn't mean having to disapprove.

• Tot up how much of the talk in your home boils down to basic instructions – "Get your coat", "Hurry up", "Time for dinner". Introducing even 10 minutes of relaxed chatter about nothing in particular (with the television off) can seem like an oasis of happy communication.

Language learning for life

Language learning does not end once a child is a fluent talker. Throughout life there are new words to learn and new subtleties of meaning to explore.

• Get her to use the powers of language she has. How did it feel to win the rounders game? If the team lost, how can they do better next time? If she wants something you are unsure about, can she convince you with her argument?

• Play creative language games. At age eight or nine, children can begin to define words. Ask her "What is a book/a banana/a bicycle?" – how precise can she be without falling back on the word itself? Try making up new expressions together: "My bed is as soft as a snowdrift"; "I'm as happy as a puppy in a meadow".

• Children always benefit from being listened to, but try to make sure her conversations are not one sided. Your child needs to be curious about others, too, ready to ask Grandad about his week rather than to simply describe her own activities. Show her how to introduce friends in a warm and lively way: "This is Joe – he's an ace goalie." This mix of confidence and generosity is what makes successful adult communicators.

" However tired I am at the end of the day she always has something to say that cheers me up. "

JESS is mum to three-year-old Zoe

Useful contacts

Afasic
2nd Floor
50-52 Great Sutton Street
London EC1V 0DJ
Tel: 020 7490 9410
Helpline: 0845 355 5577
www.afasic.org.uk
Parent-led organisation helping
children and young people with a
speech or language impairment.

**BabyCentre
(Content Consultants)**
84 Dereham Road
Easton
Norwich
NR9 5DF
Tel: 01603 882129
www.babycentre.co.uk
Information, support and guidance
on all aspects of babycare and
child development.

**British Stammering
Association**
15 Old Ford Road
London E2 9PJ
Tel: 020 8983 3591
www.stammering.org.uk
Advice and information for parents
of children who stammer.

Early Education
The British Association for Early
Childhood Education
136 Cavell Street
London E1 2JA
Tel: 020 7539 5400
www.early-education.org.uk
Support, advice and information
on the care and education of
children from 0-8 years.

I CAN
4 Dyer's Buildings
Holborn
London EC1N 2QP
Tel: 0845 225 4071
www.ican.org.uk
Services and information for
parents of children with speech
and language difficulties.

**International Association of
Infant Massage (UK Chapter)**
Tel: 07816 289788
www.iaim.org.uk

www.kidspsych.org
Interactive web site for children,
with links to child development
articles.

**National Association of Special
Educational Needs (NASEN)**
NASEN House
4/5 Amber Business Village
Amber Close
Amington
Tamworth
Staffs B77 4RP
Tel: 01827 311 500
www.nasen.org.uk
Help and support for children with
special educational needs and also
for people who work with them.

**National Association of Toy
and Leisure Libraries**
68 Churchway
London NW1 1LT
Tel: 020 7255 4600
Tel: 0131 664 2746 (Scotland)
Tel: 01874 622 097 (Wales)
www.whitetie.net/natll/

National Autistic Society
393 City Road
London EC1V 1NG
Tel: 020 7833 2299
www.nas.org.uk
Support and services for people
with autistic spectrum disorders
and their carers.

**National Deaf Children's
Society (NCDS)**
15 Dufferin Street
London EC1Y 8PD
Tel: 020 7250 0123
www.ncds.org.uk
Organization for families, parents
and carers of deaf children.

National Literacy Trust
Swire House
59 Buckingham Gate
London SW1E 6AJ
Tel: 020 7828 2435
www.literacytrust.org.uk
Charity that promotes literacy and
language skills.

**Royal National Institute for
Deaf People**
19-32 Featherstone Street
London EC1Y 8SL
Tel: 020 7296 8000
www.rnid.org.uk
Charity that represents deaf and
hard of hearing people.

www.talkingpoint.org.uk
First-stop internet site for advice on
speech, language and communication
difficulties in children for parents,
carers and educational and health
professionals.

Index

Acknowledgments

Dorling Kindersley would like to thank Sally Smallwood and Ruth Jenkinson for the photography and Sue Bosanko for compiling the index.

Illustrator Kevin Smith

Models Mark with Sophira Norr, Nick Mitchell with Oliver Saunders, Karen with Jessica and Lucy Shaw, Sasha and Isabella Velody, Pete and Shaquille Weekes, Dynia Lawrence with Tasheba and Tsehay Lee, Sharon with Dominic and Marcus Gunn, Andy with Nicholas Karamallakis, Qazi family, Quadri family, Scarlet Martin, Linda with Finn Quicke, Eve Simmonds, Michiru with Ramu Abevettath, Harvey Barron, Alex with Lola Sweeney, Anna Stennett with Lauren Ejiofor, Rita with Robin Brown, Sophia Sirius, Chris with Rebecca Halford, Nicolette with Marta Comand, Chris with Charlie Mills, Janis Lopatkin with Mia Schindler, Martine with Rose Gallie, Tom and William Orchard, Harvey Barron, Finton Reilly, Jane with Luke Rimell, Lara Peck, Babs with Damilolo and Lucas Mtfolo, Jamie Norton, Dave Mills, Jordan Townsend, Paul with Oscar Ford, Rita Agyemang, Karen with Jessica and Lucy Shaw.

Hair and make-up Victoria Barnes, Louise Heywood, Susie Kennett, Amanda Clarke

Picture researcher Anna Bedewell

Picture librarian Romaine Werblow

Picture credits

Dorling Kindersley would like to thank the following for their kind permission to reproduce their photographs:

57: Science Photo Library: James King-Holmes.

All other images © Dorling Kindersley. For further information see: www.dkimages.com